To Amber.
Wishing you the Very
Best.

Sincerely

Jake Copass—c

5/9/93

IT DON'T HURT TO LAUGH

It Don't Hurt to Laugh

COWBOY POETRY

BY JAKE COPASS

ART —— PHIL TOGNAZZINI

THE OLIVE PRESS PUBLICATIONS
LOS OLIVOS, CA 93441

© 1992 Jake Copass

Art: Phil Tognazzini

With permission Lizbeth Kyle Gallery, Los Olivos, California

Cover photo: Jake on "Doc"

Library of Congress Cataloging-in-Publication Data

Copass, Jake, 1920 -
    It don't hurt to laugh : cowboy poetry / by Jake Copass.
        p.   cm.
    ISBN 0-933380-12-7 : $10.00
    1. Cowboys--Poetry. 2. West (U.S.)--Poetry. I. Title.
    PS3553.0633218   1992
    811'.54--dc20   92-28168
                                                                CIP

Printed in the United States of America

THE OLIVE PRESS   The Olive Press Publications
Post Office Box 99
Los Olivos, CA 93441
PUBLICATIONS   Telephone/FAX: 805/688-2445

CONTENTS

CONTENTS CONTINUED

Tribute to Jake

When our family moved to the Santa Ynez Valley in the 1960s, things were much slower paced than they are in 1992. In the sleepy little town of Santa Ynez, just about the only daily activity took place in front of the post office when folks came into town to collect their mail, stop to visit, catch up on the news and learn whose livestock the coyotes had attacked, or discuss the weather and decide if it was time to cut the hay. Standing in the street to visit was absolutely no problem. If a car or pick-up happened to come by, it just drove around you and around the old black dog that slept in the street in front of the Santa Cota Market.

One of the most familiar sights was a pickup truck hitched to a goose-neck stock trailer that circulated around the valley. It was painted caution-sign yellow and if you were driving behind it, you grew accustomed to the pickup coming to a halt, the door opening, and the cowboy leaning out to spit tobacco juice on the road.

I eventually met that cowboy, and I have been enjoying Jake Copass ever since.

In the eighteen years I have been writing the newspaper column, "Woolgathering," concerning life in the valley, I have never worried about running out of material because I have always been able to call on Jake for a rare comment on life. A natural wit, Jake has the ability to make the best out of whatever life hands out. Whenever his name is mentioned, a smile appears. He personifies the term "genial," and it is no wonder he has a host of friends.

It is fitting that these poems, reflecting Jake's life and experiences, have been collected together, so that we can all have a piece of him to keep forever.

Pat Murphy
Spirit Oaks Farm, Santa Ynez, California

Jake Copass

Jake Copass, head wrangler at the Alisal Guest Ranch in Solvang, California, was born in Texas where his father contracted custom work; "hot, dusty, dry farming," according to Jake. He was one of eight children and attended a one-room school until he was in the 7th grade.

His father also raised Percherons, a breed of particularly powerful draft horses, so Jake was introduced to horses at an early age and by the time he was ten, was driving a team for $1 a day, "just like the men." When he was sixteen, he became a "Texas Cowboy," working with the 120,000 acre Pitchfork Land and Cattle Company; the herd was driven to a railhead--a four day trip.

At that time, the Pitchfork ranch had 100 hands in the summer, including 15 cowboys and a fence crew, and ran 5000 mother cows, 500 brood mares--later cut to 100--and utilized 3000 acres for winter feed. Polo ponies were also raised here. "We rode a horse for half a day, draggin' calves," Jake recalls, "then switched to a new horse, allowing them to feed on grass along the way." The ranch upgraded its stock by breeding its horses with U.S. Cavalry remount studs; in return, the Cavalry would select geldings for its own use. "We bred our horses for endurance at ranch work--heavy-boned."

During this time, Jake was breaking horses--wild mares that were not halter broken--for $20 a month plus room and board. His salary was later increased to $30.

At 17 years of age, Jake weighed less than 100 pounds-a disadvantage when it came to strength, but a definite advantage when it came to mounting a horse. "Horses are not mean," Jake insists. "What they are showing is fear. A stud horse has a protective instinct."

During WWII, Jake served in the U.S. Army and was

stationed in New Guinea. As a member of the Veterinarian Corps, he was in charge of the 1600 mules that pulled artillery into the field. "We also used pack mules for rescue work and in our searches for downed planes, but the jungle was too wet. The animals couldn't travel fast enough."

While stationed in New Guinea, Jake restructured the feeding program for the animals, making sure that all supplies were inspected and safe; a policy that was not being followed before Jake's arrival.

Jake's poem, "Great Land--No", expresses his feelings about being stationed so far from home.

In December, 1944, Jake came to Santa Barbara for two weeks R&R. The Army had established R&R camps at the Biltmore, Miramar and Mar Monte hotels where the men and their families came to relax. Jake was offered an opportunity to remain at the R&R camp and take care of the stock, and he accepted the invitation.

Jake had learned the saddle trade in the Army and after his discharge, decided to settle in Santa Barbara County. He worked at Jedlicka's which was, at the time, a shoe store. Here, he made his first saddles. After moving to the Santa Ynez Valley in 1946, he opened a shop in Solvang where he shod horses.

Jake began writing poetry in 1943, an art form that has seen a tremendous increase in popularity over the last several years. Well-known and beloved, locally, Jake is rapidly becoming a celebrity, joining other cowboy poets at gatherings in Elko, Nevada; Durango, Colorado; Lubbock, Texas and Wickenberg, Arizona.

"When you're young and you don't have much of an education," Jake told us during an interview, "you never feel like you have anything to offer anyone. Then you find out your own experiences are interesting to others."

Great Land--No

We are now thriving
  under New Guinea Skies
With those beetles
  bugs mosquitoes and flies
Where the Kangaroo, Wallaby
  and the natives grow
Where it gets plenty hot
  and it never does snow
And about the rain
  they didn't yet say.
But from the looks of the past
  it will come every day.
You are up in the morning
  at the sound of a horn
And you wish to yourself
  that you never were born.
It's then time for breakfast
  and what do you think?
Those ole powdered eggs,
  my gee how they stink
Then you fall out
  with a detail of men
And police up the ground
  till it's clean as a pen
We read books of all kinds
  about camouflage
But if you look at the place,
  you would think sabotage
All our friends back home
  with sad broken hearts

Don't realize we're here
  just building a park
We just cut everything
  and we leave the place clean
From the air from the ground,
  this camp's plain to be seen
Not one single patient
  you will finally forget
That you were such a thing
  as a Technician Vet.
Now there may come a day
  when we can do our part.
Just most anytime
  I am ready to start.
I am ready to end
  this war anytime
For I'm longing for Texas
  and that old home of mine.

                Sgt. W. Jake Copass
                March 20, 1943

Bugle Boy

At five a.m. and everything's quiet
Then the Bugle goes off with a bang.
And for some reason, can't understand why,
The poor Bugler catches the blame.

Of course he don't work like most of us do
With pick, with shovel and hoe
But if you take notice at all he does
It keeps a man right on the go.

Now soon it's time for mail call
You're sure feeling lonely and blue
You're sure hoping that ole Bugle Boy
Will bring you a letter or two.

For me, I'm sure not complaining
I'll sure never give him a growl
If he blows that Bugle till it falls apart
He's worth ninety percent for morale.

Sgt. W. Jake Copass
July, 1943

I'll be Satisfied

You can have my part of city life
With all the comforts of its kind
But I prefer the open spaces
Where the sun is sure to shine.

You can have that stuffy cottage
Down on Fifth Avenue
I'll be contented with a hut of breezes
With a roof of sky so blue.

You may have a fluffy pillow
And a fancy feather bed
I won't complain with a bed roll
With some sage brush at my head.

I guess life is what you make it
In the city, on the farm
But me I'm sticking to the country
To live and die where I was born.

Sgt. W. Jake Copass
July 27, 1943

"Dude Horse"

About five thirty a.m. at our prime sleeping time,
that's when you feel the pain;
the guys get you out of your warm sleeping place
and feed you a bucket of grain.

Now, they tie us all up to an ol' hitch'n rail,
then scratch our sore backs for a spell;
they pick at your feet, tug at your mane
and it hurts when they comb out your tail.

Then they stick the cold bridle bit in your mouth,
that's when the hurt'n really begins;
they cinch that ol' saddle in the small of your back,
which was the hide of one of your old friends!

Well, here comes some people from places uptown,
all deck out in costumes with pride;
he talks about all the places he's been
and how he really does know how to ride.

Then I really start worry'n when I hear someone say
"Will you give me a hand with this pack?"
Cause I know if it takes two people to get this guy on,
it sure can't be good for my back!!

Now, all of you ol' buddies, that's working for hay
and chasing them ol' cows out on the range;
if you're complain'n just come on by,
and I'll sure swap you jobs for a change.

1985

7

My Big Mouth

I was born in north Texas on a sandy land farm
With brothers and sisters galore
Then my Maw looked at me and said to my Paw
We shore ain't havin' no more.

Then Pay said to May, "It's really not that bad,"
As my Maw wiped off a tear
"Aw, he's just a runt and his head's sort'a big,
and his mouth is from ear to ear."

I don't know how I made it those difficult times
Through the cold, the heat, and the drought,
But I sometimes think it just might have been
On account of my dern big mouth.

November 1, 1988

True Friends

We often times neglect to think
Just what friends mean to you
But when you're at your lowest ebb
That's when they all come through.

It don't divide the rich from the poor
The brown, the black, the white.
When you think everything's all wrong
They seem to make it right.

For the caring you have shown
During sorrows of the past
Those worldly things are long time gone.
Pray my friends will always last.

November 2, 1988

Greener Pasture

I'd been riding for days through that ole mesquite brush,
Now my sides are starting to shrink.
With my jerky all gone and my alkali water
That I took from that ole water tank.

I didn't want to got back to that ole cotton patch
And be hooked to that long cotton sack,
My hands are all raw, and my shoulders all sore,
I feel like I got a broke back.

Then I spotted this cow camp in a canyon below,
I though there was a slim chance
I could sure get some water, sour dough, and some steak
To feel out the top of my pants.

The cook looks me over and he says to me, "Kid,
You seem to be ridin' alone.
I s'pose you got restless, jumped on that ole nag,
And you're probably runnin' from home."

I seys, "You're shore right, 'bout me riding alone
On that ole hoss I payed for in sweat,
As for goin' back home to that ole cotton patch,
I don't think I'm quite ready yet.

"Do you think that the Boss would give me a chance
to work on this big cattle spread?
Until I heal up, I'd do what I can
To pay for my meat, beans and bread."

Well, the Boss he says, "Son, we ain't got no time
To wet nurse a leppie like you.
But here, take his blanket and roll it out there,
We don't want you spreadin' the flu."

Awe sure got lonesome for my family back home,
Especially when times became slack.
But I never get lonesome for that sandy land farm,
Or that darned long white cotton sack.

November 5, 1988

14

Merry Christmas

I don't think I'll be writing ole Santa this year,
Don't think he'd have time to reply,
If I told him all the things I need,
He'd shrug the whole thing off with a sigh.

You don't get much for your money these days,
The Lottery buys nuthin' at all.
They just called in my Visa card
And the lay-away plan's so small.

First you get the dentist's and the doctor's bill,
one for the muddy water we drink,
Then there's the gas, the lights, the telephone,
...Property tax took care of the bank.

Some folks might say, "That's not very much,
In fact, it looks very small."
But if "O.D." on the statement is right,
You might better be making a call.

What I remember at Christmas time,
A stocking would hold everything.
An apple, an orange, some candy and nuts,
And a baseball made out of string.

If I'm lucky, I'll se the bright stars shinin',
See my friends with a big happy grin.
I'll be pleased if I find a stocking at all,
And ole Santa will fill it...again.

November 15, 1988

Brother Wes

The phone it rang, I picked it up,
'twas gettin' sorta late.
I looked up at the old timepiece,
My gosh! It's almost eight.

I said, "What's up?" It was ole Wes,
He said, "I called to say,
I think I'm over-run with folks
an' they're headed out your way!"

He said, "I tried to treat them fair.
I gave them all my food,
and now they see the cupboards bare,
They're gettin' sorta rude!"

It sure sounds bad from what you say,
I know it ain't no fun,
But thanks for callin' up in time,
It gives me time to run!

November 24, 1988

Riding Drag

I stopped at this cow camp and talked to the Cook,
"Do you think I could talk to the Boss?
I could sure use some water, a bite to eat,
And maybe trade for a fresh hoss."

"Just tie up your pony and drag up a log,
And sit by the fire a spell."
Then he moves the pot over, stirs up the fire,
Oh boy! how that hot food does smell.

Most cooks don't think kindly when grub riders drop in.
They're easy to get on the fight,
Especially at lunchtime, you're talking about,
You'ed shore like to stay for the night.

The Boss he rides up, looks all tuckered out,
Steps off that grey horse he called, "Chalk."
Could tell right off, way he's moving about,
This shore ain't no good time to talk.

Then he grabbed the horn and cheats the reins
As he steps on that ole snorty nag.
Then he hollered back, "Kid, you might as well come,
At least you can bring up the drag."

Each day, there I'd be, for the dust I can't see
Through, I poked up those doggies with pride,
All the time I'm day dreamin' when there'd be a day
I could be riding up there on the side.

First thing each night when I get back to camp,
Looking for some hungry kid on a nag,
I'm just shore hoping he's hungry enough
To take up my job riding drag.

December 2, 1988

A New Dude Hand

This Bob pulls up in his Cadillac
and steps right out with pride.
I could tell how his clothes hung on
he sure came here to ride.

His hat was new, his Levis too
and his boots all free of dung
I knew the way he started out
he could tell us how it's done.

He asks, "Is this the place to get a horse
to ride the open range?"
Went on to say how it was done
somewhere out on the plains.

I say, "That's right, that's what we do
if you've cleared it through the Boss.
I think we got one saddled up,
he's just your kind of hoss."

He says, "I shore don't want no nag
I'm not here to poke around,
I want one to really go
'cause I like to cover ground."

He said, "I never need a guide,
I always ride alone."
By then I had it figured out,
he'd never make it home.

He rushed right up to that ole hoss,
his wrong foot held up high,
I says, "If you get on that way
he'll tell us all goodbye."

"Aw, he's o.k.," I said,
"He don't really wanta fight,
he's just not used to hands like you
who mount him from the right."

I hold the stirrup and help him up
to join the other hands,
and now he starts to ride away,
still standing on my hand!

I said, "We'll start them out this way
and let them walk a spell.
Just try to keep them all in line,
just sorta head to tail."

Now o.k. I think it's time
to try a little lope,
I knew I had to stay in front,
it was my only hope.

He got down to that closed gate first,
ahead of all the rest.
But what had really happened was...
I'm sure you guess the rest.

I said, "Sir, are you o.k.?
That sure was quite a wreck.
Your shirts all torn, your Levis, too
and your hat brim's 'round your neck!"

"Aw, I'm o.k., it's not too bad,
It's really all my fault.
I thought that I could bluff it through,
and first off--I got caught."

November 25, 1988

23

Wild Cow Country

Now this kind of talk won't sound
like much to all you city folk.
But to tell those guys that went along,
they know this ain't no joke.

Now our friend Ray, he bought some cows,
boy these cows are scattered out.
All these cows that he just bought
had no plans of coming out.

He said, I'll bring you guys a horse,
you just bring your ropes and tack
'cause this country where we'll go,
it's not smooth like the track.

Now we've been out near all day
and start feeling somewhat lean,
begin to wonder if we're lost,
and not a critter have we seen.

Ray said, we'll meet up on that ridge
and have a bite to eat.
He said, the cook will meet us there,
you'll have a chance to cool your seat.

He was supposed to meet us here,
up by this old tree trunk.
But the one thing that he didn't know,
the cook he done got drunk.

The wind was picking up by then,
right down that ole jeep trail.
I think the jeep is stuck down that way,
I sorta think that's food I smell.

He says, someone can drive the jeep
to the ole tree long that crest,
we can build a fire, have a bite,
and wait there for the rest.

He said, A couple hands had gone
around that other bed,
they thought that they might find a track,
we have seen them now and then.

By then the wind was blowing hard
and was getting sorta damp.
He said, we might as well mount up
and head on back to camp.

I thought I heard somebody say,
I heard somebody yell!
Right there before my very eyes
This camp had gone to hell.

While everyone is mounting up,
some hearts filled full of glee
while some of them had done forgot
that their horses were tied to that tree.

I looked around, I sees ole Carl
as he lets out a groan.
He's trying to spur ole sorrelie up
while his hobbles are still on.

A little to my right here comes
this big ole dry fat cow.
You stuck it on her too deep Ray,
things sure gonna happen now.

I know this horse that he is on
don't know much 'bout a cow.
With them dallies tied and that big oak tree
he's just started learning now.

As he jerked the slack, he was steppin' off,
it was his only hope.
Then ole Buck, he learned a little more
when he stepped across the rope.

I said, Ray, are you okay?
As he grinned and waved at me.
Now I'm wondering what ole Buck will think
with his head drove in that tree.

Then I looked back. Buck's standing there,
he might be in a daze.
With all four feet all straddled out,
sure ain't had no time to graze.

There goes this big ole high horn cow,
bull yearling by her side,
the trail she thought that she should use
sure was no place to ride.

Now right behind her comes ole Tex,
Ray's faithful brown head dog.
He finally got her stopped up there,
behind that brush and log.

I'm now on foot and I pause a spell
to take a little blow.
I'm not too proud of my last plan,
with my horse turned loose below.

I hollered up to the other guys,
They said we're all set now.
If I miss my guess and come out first,
be sure and catch the cow.

I crawled through brush above her head
and kicked her in the snoot,
When she left, the next thing she knew
her head was in a loop.

When every one was accounted for,
it was getting might late.
If I do say so, that looks okay,
they had finally captured eight.

There was Winsor, Raymond, Lefty and Doad,
how's that sound for a start?
Yes, Link and Dutch, Brown and Hy,
you sure can't sell them short.

Yea, there's Ralph, Edmond, Cooper, too;
as Bill ride along in song.
Then there were several guys like me
who just came to tag along.

Now you'd think Channing, Bill and more,
with cameras 'round their necks,
could just have got a shot or two,
to prove we had a wreck.

As Ray and I, we head for home,
those clouds sure getting black,
he said let it pour, I feel better now,
I just filled my last contract.

December 17, 1988

29

Half Horse

I've read books and books of Equine Breeds
about shows and all their class
but I don't seem to read too much
'bout the ole long-eared Jack Ass.

Awe, I have seen them pull a cart,
a wagon and a plow,
But low and behold, I can't believe
some folks, they ride them now.

Now I don't know much 'bout this mule
or how he came about
but it don't take him very long
to have you figured out.

Awe, he'll do his work as he knows best,
just give him half a chance.
I got a feeling if you don't,
you're done kicked in the pants!

Now you may poke and jab him 'round,
and say he's just a fool,
but what I've seen, just standing by,
you sure don't know this mule.

Now you say, "Ole mule, I got you now!"
as you whip him out alone.
Next thing you think, while getting up,
"That mule's done gone back home."

Now like I say, I don't know much,
but if you want my a'vise;
if you want that mule to do his part,
you might better treat him nice.

January 5, 1989

Short Handed

My friend call up an' he said Jake
Could you come give us a hand?
We could use the help if you have the time
We got some calves to brand.

When I got there I knows I'm late
'cause the sky has done turned red,
I ask the boss, where's all the help?
Hell, they must still be in bed.

They finally started showing up,
By then the sun is shining bright
but before they get those pickups stopped,
done had a good dog fight.

They seem to come from everywhere,
sorta stop like riding skids,
by the time that ole cowboy's out,
here comes the wife and kids.

By the time that they're all saddled up,
I'm sure it must be eight,
'bout then I heard somebody say,
"Let's have a coffee break!"

Well, they finally started drifting out,
some strung out far behind,
some a sorta running out sideways,
I don't counted forty nine.

'Bout then some fellow galloped by,
He said, "Now ain't this fun?"
I said we sure should get 'em in
Looks like it's two to one.

January 5, 1989

Good Ole Days

"It's almost four," my Dad would say,
Of course we knew the rule,
You better get those Jerseys milked
And don't be late for school.

When you go out now don't forget
To take along a saw
Cut that ice out of that water trough
'cause it's sure not gonna thaw.

Now don't forget to slop the hogs
and feed the horses maize
It seems I've heard some folks say
"They were the good ole days."

My older sisters head for school
Like going to a race
And me, I'm trotting close behind
So the snow won't hit my face.

They'd say, "Come on it's not to far,
It's just a little ways."
I wasn't interested very much
about those good ole days.

You get back home your warmed up some
And your feeling sorta good.
'bout then you hear your mother say
"It's time to get in the wood."

Then you feed the hogs and milk the cows
As you squat there in a daze
Now knowing that you're really part
Of all those good ole days.

Now at supper time we'd gather round
for that cornbread, milk and beans.
And for me I can't forget
Those home canned Turnip Greens.

Now I know these day's that things have changed
in many, many ways
And I still shiver when I think
about those good ole days.

January 6, 1989

36

City Rancher

The guy moves in just down the road
Thinks he bought the ranch for fun.
But it really wasn't very long
He could tell you how it's done.

No matter what ole timers say
They think there's not a chance.
But I know there's money to be made
The way I'll run this ranch.

He said how he had gone to school
To learn the modern way
He said he had it figured out
How this ole ranch will pay.

Thirty sections in that computer box
Has it all figured out.
I sure won't need those Cowboys 'round
To run my herd about.

Four hundred cows they won't eat much
I can always feed them hay.
And when they all come down to eat
I can see them every day.

Now he stopped by to chat a spell
I could see some sign of pain
Is there a chance from that blue sky
That we could get a rain?

He crawled up on that three wheel bike
He says I guess I'll go
Because I said don't know about rain
But we sure could get some snow.

It didn't seem like many months
Then I seen the banker pass
I just supposed he's going up
To help him count his cash.

Now he calls up went on to say
How much he loves this life
But said he had to move to town
On accountin' of his wife.

The IRS man he just stopped by
He asked if there's a chance
If there was someone I might know
Who would like to buy this ranch.

January 9, 1989

Wild Horse Race

My friend Tony said to me
I hoped you'd understand
We're going to a Wild Horse Race
And we need a good shank man.

It's not too bad, as he talked on,
Think he gave me some false hope.
I'm sure you'll handle it okay
You're pretty handy with a rope.

I said sure and why not
As we headed on our way
Four hundred miles down the road
For a rodeo that next day.

Now I looked in that bucking chute
At that spotted popeyed brute,
Don't look like that's no easy way
To make a lot of loot.

Ole Spot he come right out that cage
Like he's marching in a band,
Before I knew that red hot shank
Done buzzing through by hand.

He jumped astraddle all of us
As though he was a tank,
And both those guys a'screaming, "JAKE!
Just don't let go that shank!"

I didn't know how long it took
to get that saddle on,
Then I heard someone say,
He's mounted up and gone.

Well, they finally got me all propped up
Against that bucking chute,
Bout then ole Tony just went by
Still pounding on that spotted brute.

Now they said, "It's all your fault!"
I know I'm gonna faint.
"Because you wouldn't let him go,
You'se still holdin' on that shank."

Now I'm not known for being smart,
But there's one thing I do understand,
The next Wild Horse Race that I see
I'll be seein' it from the stands.

I bet the next hand that you ask
You will probably stop and think
Could he be one more green horn
To have trouble with that shank.

January 13, 1989

Horse Trainer Wanted

I need a hand to run my ranch,
He must be diversified,
You will sure be your own boss,
Just run the place with pride.

Of course your wife will tend our house
Help wifie with the guests.
I'm sure that she will have the time
To keep my good suits pressed.

We already have three cows to milk,
For our pigs we mix the slop,
And we have a bunch of laying hens
In a pen behind the shop.

Now I'm sure you have a set of tools
To make that tractor run.
I bet you like to tinker 'round;
To me, it's always fun.

Irrigation system's figured out;
We change them twice a day,
We always seem to work it in
While puttin' up the hay.

Another thing I forgot to say,
Thought we'd better talk about,
There's one thing I just can't have,
Some kids who run about.

Now all these colts are halter broke,
Have to take it sorta slow,
I think we got a full two months
Before we have a show.

We got that little house back there,
That sits up on those hills.
Of course I know you understand
You pay all the electric bills.

On Sundays we may not be home,
We just might stay in town;
But just in case someone drops by,
I know you'll be around.

January 27, 1989

Ants in Your Bed

Did you ever lay down in your ole bed roll
to get much needed rest
Just to be woke up in a little while
in the middle of a red ants nest?

Bare foot you hobble through the thorns
Pull your bed out to the side
Soon you find out, that don't help
You just gave those ants a ride.

Then you hear some ole cowboy say
"Kid why don't you be quiet?
Them damn ants they won't eat much
You just got them on the fight."

You think you might as well get up.
It seems your only chance
It don't take long to figure out
There's more roosting in your pants.

Now all of you young Waddies
Just remember what I said...
You better do some scouting
Before rolling out your bed.

Now if you think I'm fooling
Go on and take the chance
But don't be howlin'out for help
When those red ants are in your pants!

February 8, 1989

43

"Guest Breakfast Ride"

In the wee hours, I'm up and I'm stumbling around
As I feel for the switch by the door,
Stumble over my boots tangled up in my pants,
Then I find myself flat on the floor.

I finally get dressed and I hurry outside,
Find my keys, I'm not havin' much luck,
All those floodlights shining in my face,
I walk slap dab into my truck.

Oh Lord, "It's got to get better"
I lowes I best not be late,
Sure can't miss that breakfast ride,
We got to be ready by eight.

Well I finally shows up, though I barely can see,
It looks like a terrible sight.
All those folks hanging on the ole top rail
They must have been waiting all night.

Now I grab a saddle for that snorty ole nag,
I'm half asleep he sure can tell,
But all of a sudden I sure wake up
As he kicks me across the corral.

As I look around, I figures this out,
No time to be cussin' out loud,
As, it's just something we always do,
Just a little sideshow for the crowd.

Now you waddies just get mounted up,
I hope the whole trip is amusin'
But if you're like me and that sore back horse,
You'll only have pain and confusion.

September 30, 1989

Western Swing

Now it might have always been that way
Or maybe 'cause I'm getting older,
'Bout all the pleasures that you have
Is in the eyes of the beholder.

I remember the nights when chores were done,
We'd sit around the ole wood fire,
Then my momma she'd walk in
with her Sears and Roebuck guitar.

We sat there by those coal oil lights,
Try to learn to read the songs,
All eight kids would join right in
As my momma strummed along.

My dad was always telling tales
And the rest is acting silly,
It didn't really bother much,
Having folks call us "hillbilly."

Do you suppose in this day and time,
If we were to sit around and sing,
Is there a chance some folks might say,
"That sounds like Western Swing."

December 31, 1989

48

Stranger in Town

I'm not sure this is the place
For a stoved up hand like me,
But thought I might just try it once,
Since I saw it on TV.

One thing I've learned this far from home,
Shore don't want to cause no fuss,
They might not give a guy a chance,
To catch the Greyhound Bus.

The Cowboys used to come to town
To some all night Honky Tonk
To have a drink and boast about
He's the best at busting broncs.

He used to pack a gun around
And did a lot of fitten'
But now he packs a briefcase
filled with poetry he's written.

I once heard somebody say,
"Yea think he's a 'dallie' man?
You know it's sorta hard to tell,
Has all his fingers on his hand.

"Guess he might be a 'hard and fast'
From some ranch out on a flat,
He might be off a chicken farm
With all those feathers on his hat."

Now some might say he's spreadin' bull,
And most times could be true,
But this ain't the time to spread it out
On lovely folks like you.

Now I hope you folks are not hostile,
And will let me off the hook,
If I get by with this episode,
I might even write a book!

January 13, 1990

Jima Red

I'd been riding some colts
on the outskirts of town
at fifty a month and their hay.
Got it all figured out,
I can't pay the bills,
Have to make some more money some way.

Then a neighbor comes by
and sez with a grin,
There's something you might think about.
Jim's got a roan filly,
she's cranky somewhat,
They gone up and just turned her out.

Well I'm new in these parts
but I thought to myself,
Might give me a good chance to brag.
Thought I'd just saunter over
and have me a look
Might be able to trade for that nag.

I'd heard a few stories
about this roan mare
It's hard to tell at first glance.
I said to myself, she can't be too bad,
Just don't think they gave her a chance.

II

Now I'm not very sharp
When you talk pedigree,
But she looks pretty well bred
With those good muscled legs
and a nice short back,
She sure packs a nice little head.

I kicked some dirt up under her chin
in the corral as she come running by.
I said to the foreman do you think she's for sale?
He sez I couldn't care less if she'd die.
I no more than got home than the telephone rang,
Was ole Jim on the end of the line.
Just talked to the foreman, he said you come by
and you liked that roan filly of mine.

He says she's got papers of a Waggoner mare
by a horse they call him Driftwood.
All the time I am thinking, for two hundred bucks
This Jima Red's got to be good.

Now first thing right off, don't want you to think
I'm that rough string tough Buckaroo,
But I just couldn't wait to get this little roan home,
'Cause I did have an idea or two.

III

I pulled out her mane, cleaned out her tail
She sure stood there hobbled quite well,
I'll have her gentle in a little while,
I know she'll be easy to sell.

I pulled off the hobbles and turned her around,
My saddle all cinched down tight.
She just walked off, not trouble at all,
I done lost my feeling of fright.

She moves right out as we go back and forth
across that big ole corral.
And all of a sudden, something must have gone wrong,
'Cause I'm don bucked off on my tail.

Yep, we'd be working cattle, some smart aleck would say,
Jake, can't you get that ornery steer out?
It's not that steer that's bothering me much,
It's this roan filly I'm worried about.

After seven long years, thought the time never come
I'd be able to brag on that nag,
With a twist in my neck, my arm in a sling,
And a three-foot-long cast on my leg.

One day ole Pat pulled in and sez to me Jake
I hear you have a Waggoner Driftwood
I have some people that's wanting to buy,
They'll pay but she's got to be good.

Now for twelve hundred bucks,
after all those years,
For then it only seemed fair
I never could brag on that filly of mine
But Pat has a good cranky ole mare.

March 15, 1990

53

"Here's the Fire"

Finally get the crew together
And all the cattle in the pen
But you ain't seen the half of it
With all those cow folks ridden in.

They said us--Get the cows out
Shore don't sit around and wait
It's sorta hard to get them critters
With half those cow folks in the gate.

By now they start the roping
As you stand there somewhat a'feared,
Now you start to look around
You see all the ground crew's disappeared

Aw sure they get doggies roped
Like some western movie star,
But somewhere in the process,
They ain't found out where's the fire.

By now they get another caught,
Getting there you're out of breath,
Don't suppose it really matters now,
He's done almost choked to death.

Do you think they might be bashful?
Or maybe they just forgot,
I think this branding iron's cold now,
Since I pack the thing a block.

Now I'd like to get him branded,
But I sure don't need no lip,
He can kick there now till doomsday,
Without this brand up on his hip.

Sure some might say he's cranky,
He'd be better I'm sure by far,
If you'd get that little critter
Somewhere closer to the fire.

If you seem to get a deaf ear
From the ground crew 'cross the lot,
They all seem to hear much better
When you drag him to the pot.

Didn't learn too much 'bout brandin' calves,
Probably most all I forgot,
But just seems to work lots better
A little closer to the brandin' pot.

April 18, 1990

56

Little Liz

I just stopped past the ole flag pole
In this Los Olivos town,
Just two blocks off one fifty four
And I start to look around.

Across the street sez Western Art
I laws I'll just drop in,
Thought I'd have myself a peek
Might bump into a friend.

Art on the floor, some on the wall
Some pieces big and some are small
There's pencils, water, oil and wood
It all looked good from where I stood.

I wondered where the owner's at
Can't be her under that slouchy hat
She sez "That's me. I can explain,
I've just been working on a picture frame."

Her hair is blonde, her eyes are blue,
I'd guess her height at five foot two.
She's not too big, still not too thin,
Don't make much difference with that cute grin.

By now you've forgot about Western Art,
Overcome by this sudden thrill,
She speaks right up, "My name is Liz.
The big guy's my husband Bill."

July 10, 1990

Mr. Shoofly

I said who's this feller Shoofly?
I hear so many talk about.
Met him a short time later,
But still couldn't figure it out.

Now some sez he's from the city,
Makes no difference, I suppose,
Something I seem to like about him--
Maybe his boots and Western clothes.

He's shore not much for talkin'
But he has a friendly grin,
He does a lot of settin' 'round,
With a big ole scratch pad and a pen.

Though he might be counting cattle,
As there were some trotting by,
Thought he just might be the foreman,
This feller they call Shoofly.

Found out he's not too shabby
At catching doggies now and then,
He's durned shore apt to catch you, too,
With that camera in his hand.

An ol' cowpoke, he does fancy drawing
At the show at the Pepper Tree,
I just saw one at Liz's place--
Heck, that thing looks a lot like me.

I've known this feller for some time, now,
Yep--I still see him now and then,
I sure think I'm might lucky
Having Julie and Shoofly for my friends.

July 10, 1990

Feeling Fine Now

I wash my teeth with Ajax
Make 'em shine with Efferdent,
Under arms I use some KRS
For my terrible body scent.

On my head I use some mink oil
For that little hairy spot,
It's not designed to grow more,
But might shine the few I got.

Seems my hearing is getting weaker,
And my eyes are fadin' too
Now my mind it's 'bout stopped thinking,
'Bout the things I'm sposed to do.

My poor ole legs don't track too well
Fell they're almost out of place,
Don't suppose it really matters,
Shore don't have no one to chase.

Then I eyes this little missie
She might help me warm the bed,
Got to thinking 'bout the price tag,
Bought a heating pad instead.

Now the Doc just looked me over
Says your troubles are so small,
I just might have one suggestion
Double up on the Geritol.

August 22, 1990

61

Viking Cowboy

Did I hear you say Danish Cowboy?
Who heard of such a durn thing?
Next thing you gonna be telling me
This guy can play Western swing.

I've known a lot of good Cowboys
Somehow I thought most were the same
Till I bumped into this young feller
This nice Viking Cowboy, a Dane.

Some sey you got to be joking
Some sey it cannot be true
I'll sure be the first at Confession
This Bob is some tough Buckaroo.

Yep, he just got bucked off this morning
And landed slap dab on his head
He sez its gotta be better 'n sleeping late
Cause most folks are dying in bed.

He can take an ole hoss that's sure salty
A few days he's got him sure broke
Rope an ole wild cow on the rim rock
Have her tied to an ole scrubby oak.

He's not only a mighty good Cow man
And helps so many people in need
There's just something 'bout this old Cowboy
One of the few that's left of the breed.

I'm the type of guy that don't miss the chance
To give an old friend a dig
But there's one thing we got to agree
We all love that guy we call Sig.

October 30, 1990

64

Cowboy's Hat

I tell you one thing about waddies I've known
If you want to get fur in the fat
It's never no never, what ever you do
Don't mess with an ole Cowboy's Hat!

He might sleep on this saddle, leaned up 'ginst a tree,
Stretched out on this ground like a cat
And you better be careful if you're walkin' by
'cause he shore ain't asleep in his hat.

He'll loan you his bridle, his blanket or spurs
His chaps, his gloves or his bat,
His rope or his hobbles, but there's not a chance
That you could ever borrow his hat!

You can spook his ole pony and run him away,
Pack his bed roll way out on the flat
But you better stay clear for a couple of days.
And damn shore don't fool with his hat!

December 3, 1990

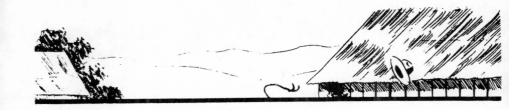

Pedigree

We were sitting on the bunkhouse steps
And one ol' cowboy said to me
You been braggin' 'bout them broomtails,
What about your pedigree?

Well, I know I'm some part Okie,
A lot of Texan, I suppose,
Think my mama's folks came from England--
Just what that is, I shore don't know.

Some say they could be blueblood,
Don't think that's a terrible sin,
Think I remember mama saying
Some Indian blood might have got mixed in.

Seems my papa's folks came from Ireland,
Lived in those old Kentucky hills,
He could be some part moon shiner
Raised among those skinners stills.

It would be hard to find some papers
of a fancy pedigree,
Don't suppose it really matters
'Cause what you see is only me.

January 1, 1991

The Chore Boy

Most every rancher has one,
He's somewhat a different scamp.
But the Boss don't always notice
The things he's doing 'round the camp.

He never gets top wages,
Though he'd never tell you so,
But you could always borrow money
If you had some place to go.

He gathers eggs and feeds the chickens,
Milks that ornery kicking cow,
And he always plants a garden
With a mule and walking plow.

He can fix a broke-down tractor
Yes, he'll wash the Boss's dogs,
And he'll never ask no questions
When he's told to butcher hogs.

He'll go out and mend the fences,
Never once her him complain,
Be the one to feed the livestock,
When it snows or pouring rain.

He'll come in and help cook breakfast,
Then shine up the kitchen floors.
Soon he's off with the cook apron,
Back at doing all his chores.

If you need an extra Cowboy,
He's mighty good and'll never peep.
All the hands are in the bunkhouse,
He's out pinnin' up the sheep.

When the time comes and he's drifted
To his final resting place,
Seems it always takes three fellows,
To take the Chore Boy's place.

February 7, 1991

Stick Horse Race

I'm sure you've heard lots of stories
'Bout the Cowboy and the West,
But this one's a little different,
All 'bout me and brother, Wes.

Now he's four and I am seven,
And I knows it must be true,
I shore had a lot more practice,
Bein' a stick horse buckaroo.

I sure got a fancy pony,
A broomstick stored behind the door,
Now ol' Wes, he's on a thoroughbred
out of a ten-foot, two-by-four.

I'm out early now, I'm training,
As I gallop down and back,
Just to have a little knowledge
On this fancy stick horse track.

Now I knows I'll be the starter
As I turns ol' broomstick 'round,
We're off and ol' Thoroughbred stumbles--
Brother Wes, he's on the ground.

Sounds like Wes is sure unhappy
As he lets out a terrible moan--
Then I found out sometime later
He had broke his shoulder bone.

It's been so many years now,
Still have some feeling of remorse,
Wes, on his two-by-four Thoroughbred--
Me, on my fancy broom.

March 21, 1991

It's Always Home

We all drove down the old dirt road,
My sisters, my brothers, and me.
It wasn't too easy to figure it out,
Where the old home used to be.

Guess the old house had been torn down,
The windmill and the old corral
The little tin chicken house is still standing there
In the brush, there is still a dim trail.

You could hear the Bobwhites in the distance,
Cows munching grass up to their knees,
I'd swear that's the same old mockingbird
Perched high in that old apple tree.

No matter what else has happened,
There's some things you cannot erase,
The joys we all had together,
On our folk's little sandy-land place.

August 25, 1991

74

Out for Breakfast

It didn't sound too tough to me. After all, you didn't have to show up until six o'clock (a.m, that is). Nothing to getting a few folks up on some gentle ol' hoss for a breakfast ride into the hills. You feel like you have done your share at scraping off the old sweat from the day before and getting fifty saddles on. You should be ready to load up by seven thirty.

Listening to a conversation between the head wrangler and a guest, however, it becomes clear that we have sixty folks attempting to mount fifty heads of horses. Another thing that seems clear is that two-seated saddles are not a common piece of equipment on this particular spread.

It would seem fair to say that many folks headed in the same direction would have about the same thing in mind concerning what is taking place. Perhaps the age group from seven to seventy could change somewhat; one thing for sure, they are all ready for the action to commence. I guess a fellow can get a bit touchy that early in the morning on an empty stomach.

The wrangler's first question seems reasonable enough. "I guess all you folks are signed up to ride?"

"Not yet," was one quick reply. "That's what we are here for. No one told us we should sign up in advance. Can we have our horses now? You seem to have plenty of them."

"No sir. The ones that are signed up for aren't in the corral yet."

"Here. Would all you folks please read and sign the release papers? Be sure and check one the box indicating your riding ability and your room number."

75

"Please," says one gentleman as he starts through the gate. "I don't need a release. I have been riding all my life. My folks have always had horses." He is handed a release slip. "What's that? Something else to sign?"

"It's only thirty dollars," the wrangler assures him as he picks up the four clip boards that have fallen off the fence. "No charge if you are on the R.U.V. Program."

"What's that?"

"That's where the horseback riding is included in your charges."

"Oh, I don't know if we are or not. If we are not on the plan, scratch five of us. Which five? The two of us plus those three children over there on those horses. We will go up on the hay truck."

Another handful of forms comes into view. "Where do we get our horses?"

"Just inside the corral. Your name should be on the blackboard by your horse's name and number. One of the wranglers inside will give you a hand." (The wranglers are those wearing the dirty boots and slouchy hats.)

By now, the little tots have shown up; you can see their little heads and their hands sticking through the fence as they attempt to pet the horses. On the legs, of course. I think the good Lord is giving us a little help about now.

As you walk over, hoping to discourage some of the hands sticking through while attempting to get a horse for another ride, someone calls from across the fence. Seems the sign-up wrangler just about has had all the questions he can handle. Holding a shivering child, one mother has several questions. "What time does the hay ride leave? Where do we get on? Is there any charge for the wagon ride? Can we take the baby? Don't you have a horse that the little ones can ride while waiting?" (As if I were waiting!)

I'm sure I heard the next question correctly.

"Could we have a private ride? We don't want to ride with a large group. Some of them might not go fast enough. We are all good riders."

Yep. There's a lot of one-sided planning going on outside the corral, but it's not getting the ride out much faster. "Sir," I ask the next gentleman, "what horse are you riding?"

"Don't know," is his reply.

"Is your name on the blackboard?"

"What blackboard?"

"The one on the tack room door, behind all those folks that are watching the magpies on the roof overhead."

"It's not here!"

"I'll try to find you a horse." (I hope. But how?) "Which of the three rides were you planning on?"

"The Breakfast Ride," he states with pride. ("That seems fair enough," I say to myself, "since Breakfast Rides are all we are having.")

"Which of the three Breakfast Rides would you like to go on?"

"Oh. I thought there was only one ride."

"We have a ride for the experienced on which will be doing a great deal of loping or cantering," I explain; "an intermediate on which will be doing some loping; then we have as slow ride for the novices."

"What is a lope?" he wonders.

"It is the same as a gallop."

"Can't we do a little loping on the novice ride? I don't want to just walk all the way."

"Are you signed up as a good to average rider," I ask.

"I'm not sure," he answers, looking over the fence toward his wife for support. "Honey, which ride are we going on?" (I am sure she had just gone through the same conversation with another wrangler.)

"Try the intermediate," she tells him. "You can make it okay. All you have to do is hold onto the horn. These horses know where they are going. I am sure they have been there many times before."

"Will I need an extra coat?" (Not if he is as worked up over this ride as I am.)

"I will go with my wife," he decides. "I sure want a horse that will keep up but won't go too fast for me."

It's not easy, when you weigh only 140 pounds, to hoist a 200-pound man up on a sixteen-hand horse, especially when he is standing on your thumb--stuck in the stirrup by mistake during your attempt to get him on top of the horse.

Ah yes. An elbow between the eyes--his elbow, your eyes.

"What are these?" he asks. Good question for a loper. "Bridle reins. They are used when you wish to turn and stop this critter."

"Ah! I guess you can see I don't do this everyday."

This fact had occurred to me earlier.

"I'm beginning to wonder," he says, "perhaps I'm not qualified for the intermediate ride."

"Perhaps," I say to myself, "a little prayer is in order."

"We haven't even started to ride yet," he continues. "I don't feel like breakfast. And I think my heart is acting up."

December 28, 1989

Cowboy Training School

Being born on a sandy-land cotton farm in the middle of ranching country sure puts a fellers mind to thinking at a pretty young age. Chopping that cotton and pulling the cotton sack sure makes a feelers shoulder sore; 'specially when my dad expected me to put more cotton in that sack so he could haul it to market.

There was some mention about going to the little two-room schoolhouse a few miles down the road. That didn't sound too good, either. I laws I could get just about all the education I would need riding one of those nice ranch horses. However, there is a little education involved in being a cowboy, too. And I see, right off, these fellers that's going to do the teaching is a lot more eager to give a button a hand in getting started (or so I thought).

"First thing off," sez one oldtimer, "no up and coming young cowboy can wear a pair of tennie shoes with no strings." Also, "He would be willing to sacrifice a pair of boots for a good cause."

Of course, there was no mention they were number nines to fit a number five foot. Yep. They're shined up, somewhat, and has a small hole in the sole about the size of a silver dollar.

"Aw, that don't show like a pair of tennie shoes with no strings. Besides, they got tall tops, green, too. The rattlers might think they're grass and won't bite a chunk out of your leg."

Yes. Stowing those boots in the corner of the bunkhouse didn't help any after the stitching in the spur pieces was worn out. And no one but me, and that nice feller that gave them to me, knows that those sharp spur pieces in the heels are going to be eating on my ankles pretty good.

Ol' Cookie--he's a lot of help, too. Bragging 'bout all that fine work I'm doing, digging the firepit in that pile of rocks. Yes--and dragging all that wood into camp. "Need plenty wood. Could be won't be any at next camp, ten miles up the way."

I am becoming a little concerned by night, with those spur pieces chewing at my ankles. But another one of my good buddy's laws, "If they aren't better by tomorrey, I can put a little KRS on them when we start branding calves."

"Might help if you soak them feet in the dish water when you get the dishes washed after supper," sez Red. "That lye soap is good for things like that."

There's one thing about these good ol' cowboy teachers--they always want a kid to be comfortable at night. He might even brag on you a bit if he thinks he can talk you into putting his heavy bed roll on the wagon next morning.

The cook? If he chooses, he can afford to be a little cranky. And most times, he chooses. But there's one thing you have to remember--you got to go past him to get to that chuck box.

Another thing was sorta hard to figure out. You have your bedroll all rolled out, your boots and pants off, and you are now informed that--on a hundred and twenty thousand acres--you have your bedroll slap dab on the wagon boss's place.

So, through the thorns I drag my bed, hoping not to get someone else's place. 'Bout now, I am doing a little thinking on my own. Sorta like taking one of those chuck wagon mules that's staked out and heading back to headquarters. The only thing is, with no moon, which way is headquarters? It is difficult to understand why a kid would get lost after all that good advice I had been getting from all of my teachers.

So I hump up in my bedroll with a few silent whimpers 'cause I sure don't want someone calling me a crybaby. Soon, I fall off to sleep.

It's amazing how good it can make a kid feel, next morning about four, to have the wagon boss walk by, ruffle up your shoulders, and ask how you rested at "The Waldorf Astoria" last night.

And what happened to Cookie during the night? Said he had some warm water he didn't need to make coffee-- thought it might shine those freckles a little.

Somehow, ol' Red found some paper to chink up my boots. Even found some extra cotton. The wrangler even come up with some cotton. "Might keep them spur pieces from eatin' yur feet off. Sure can't use no crippled help t'day. That ol' nag yur ridin' is bad 'nough." Handing me a bridle, he sez with a grin, "Us go wrangle hosses. Nobody else 'round this outfit but me and you knows anythin' 'bout wranglin' hosses."

1990